Leaf River

Poems By

Samone Norsworthy

Happy Birthday
to my very
beautiful niece!
LOVE,
Auntie
10/05

Protea Publishing

Protea Publishing Company. USA
email: kaolink@msn.com
web site: www.proteapublishing.com

First Edition Worldwide

ISBN 1-931768-33-1 soft cover

ISBN 1-931768-34-x hardcover

Library of Congress Control Number: 2002103366

Poetry is my solace of soul.
The only place my heart feels whole.

S. Norsworthy

For Matthew

On Childhood is dedicated to my beautiful girls, Georgia and Charlotte.

Acknowledgments

Grateful acknowledgment is made to *KotaPress Poetry Journal* in which "Faith" was first published. Acknowledgment is given for the guidance and critique of my writing to the professors at Armstrong Atlantic State University, in particular, Mr. William Martin, Mr. John Welsh, Dr. Chris Baker, Dr. Martha Marinara and Dr. Rich Raymond. Special acknowledgment is given to Dr. Debi McEniry for the inspiration to chase a dream. I'd like to express gratitude to the staff of *The Calliope*, the members of Sigma Tau Delta, The Masquers and Dr. Peter Mellen.

Special thanks for inspiration to: my husband Matthew, my children Georgia and Charlotte, my parents Frank & Charlotte, my brother & sister Melvin & Kyndall, my cherished friends Mondie & Meg. "Ode to Mildred" is dedicated to Mondie Gagliardo and "A Day for Resolution" is dedicated to Meg Albertson.

Contents

On Life

On Life

Leaf River

Mind wanders
turbulently to no avail
while the wind whispers
silently across the leaf river.

Mind wanders for meaning.

Listen to the rapture
of leafless life and
ponder its mortal magnificence.

Gray grows the tree.

Grow old in the pasty shell
of flesh while the mind wanders.
Enthrall in the delight
of waking in paralyzed fashion
to a semiconscious mind
that ruminates mortality.

Question the meaning
of the whistling howl of the soul.

Despise the terror
of the righteous curse
that leads one down the leaf river.

The leaves rustle as the mind ponders.

The season has bestowed

a final blow as the
paralyzed mind wanders.

Louder and louder the howl.

Quicker and colder the wind.

Frail in mortal flesh
as the mind rides
the whispering wind
across the leaf river.

Fall's glorious warning
is faintly noticed
as the mind holds
contempt, the
gray tree.

Morning Coffee

Over an antique oak table
I sit with paper in hand
and read daily fables
of a charming southern land.

Thoughts of plans for the day
litter my mind to mist
while the hammock calls to lay
and I push back the list.

Outside the sun begins its birth
and awakens the creatures
who join themselves to the earth
as bird parents become teachers.

My morning cup sits along side
my outstretched and empty arms
that grasp for more time to hide
from the chores of daily, life alarms.

The Railing

The only thing that prevents me from falling face first in a swan-like dive onto the black and white marble floor thirty-three feet below is a complex gathering of twisted iron held together by welds.

Its cascading arms drip into incomplete circles laced together for fashion's sake. It's careful not to block the view in such a way as to constantly remind me that danger is just past this wrought iron railing.

Benevolence

Watch intently
the sharpened arrow
of a silent smirk.

Listen with careful,
guarded ear the
faint whispers of mistrust.

Doubt the earnest.
Learn with sharpened
mind and hallowed heart.

Those who conquer benevolence
are most unnoticed, opposing
the obvious miserable creatures.

Know that once one
places misguided trust
in the hallow shell of benevolence,
the heart is wounded
with a fierce and fiery blow
that echoes eternity.

Befriend oneself as true friend.
Befriend oneself as only friend.

An Actor's Confession

What gets me angry is simplicity,
the simple barking of a fenced
dog after midnight that makes me
lie awake and count my pulse.

I lay under the goose down comforter
and act like I'm asleep. Just like I
acted like I didn't care when my
boss cursed me and made me feel
like a complete idiot, asking what's
the difference between qualitative
and quantitative. Give me a break!

I can't sleep, so I think. I think about
the many times I've had to act in my life.
I place on my Greek mask and become
a character. In most cases, I act like
I'm not something, embarrassed,
horrified, hurt, angry, and in some
cases happy.

The dog barks are followed now by
short howls that rip through the
black air and pierce my thoughts.

I act like it doesn't bother me –
that way I don't have to do something
about it. That's me in a nutshell.
Acting is an everyday, always on

improvisational journey that
instinctively occurs when
something goes wrong.

Accents

Whilst I ponder the thickness of speech, I am in awe
at the sound.

This language born out this small isle causes visitors
to ruminate in wonder of this other world where
people talk senseless words without sound.

The trolley is not what you would think, nor the chips
and biscuits.

The tube is monstrous,
but not what I define a tube to be;
neither the shag, the nag,
nor the candlestick maker.

The market, the districts, the gardens and such faintly
resemble ones we know.

The parks, vast and green with funny grass that never
grows where we grew.

The cars rumble with a gurgling sound that echoes off
ancient smutty buildings.

A brief experience on this great isle creates accents
and memories that stay the while.

Flight

Quiet.
Chirping, chirping.
Adolescent fowl in tangled nest
chirping.
Stumbling child of winged beasts chirping.
Silence.
Flight.

Freedom

Set free, this once
caged human feels light

floating through life
without the binding chains
men placed on her
to hold her down.

Struggling ceases to
future unknowing.

She coasts with leisure,
harnesses thrown to the
wild and untamed wind.

She will never be
second again.

Middle Management

Middle management $50k'ers
are destined to monotony like
little rats scurrying on the
running wheel and going nowhere.
Sad. Ridiculous.
As was I, but no more.

London

Clean air. No. Not quite, but crisp and unique.
The age and wonder that one feels encompasses the
view and gives comfort to visitors.

I would like to stay for a while if I could, but time has
torn me, and made me miss another across the wide
mysterious water.

She waits, so innocent, for me to return and I wish she
could join me here, away, far away from the
nothingness of there.

I'll return to my home one day.
I'll be in London forever to stay.

The Seduction

Some software company is here -
obviously - and booked all the
meeting rooms. Scores of dark
suited cell phone users dot the lobby.

All of them sickening in their
obnoxious self-importance.
Promises of emails and be-in-touches
cloud the air while me, in my jeans
and white linen blouse pity them,
these faces without names known only
by social security numbers.

Trivial, all of it. They are seduced
by the emptiness of corporate intrigue.

Lost

I've lost them.
Searching . . .
they cannot be found.
Years and years of words
feelings and experiences
lost forever.
Only in my heart they remain.

Summer Off

This is the first time
for freedom.
Time to think.
Time to rot.

Work? No.
Patience? Maybe.
On and on one goes.
Work, home, sleep
until now.
No job.
Summer off.

Useless? Maybe.
Mother first.
Wife too.
Professional? No longer.

This is the first time
for freedom.
Questionable.

Game of Pleasantries

A gray mist forms into cat fur atop a bed of
crumpled newspapers with ink circled
want adds.

The telephone is glued to my ear.
My chair, once a restful place, has
become wrought with hard surfaces
that jab without apology.

"I'm not sure when we're coming home,"
I tell the listener, knowing full well
I want to move back home
to Savannah.

"Christmas is a possibility." I
search for ways to politely escape
telling how I really feel. "Sure, we'll come
home for Christmas." I answer the
sincere beaconing.

I place the phone back on its ivory
plastic wall mount. They miss
me as I do them: so begins the
game of pleasantries. Bitter;
I became of it all and moved away.

My mistake. I stand, stretch and saunter
over to my piano and play,
not for the love of sound,

but for the love its honesty.

Vanity

To what do we owe thy great presence?
With regal countenance and pride, you enter the room.

Broad shoulders, straight spine, gaping grin.
The room hushes as your essence stifles the air.

Onlookers are awestruck with wonder and envy.
None seek the honesty that my truth shall bring.

See there! See there! He's lead by a string.
No greatness, no honor, or valor owned is he:

just ruthlessness, shame and vanity!

Contents

It has an odd shape.
Fat bottomed, skinny topped
and hollow. Strangely, it
holds one tall dried flower
and one short lid-lipped bulb.
Grey glazed and dripped black,
this structure is fascinatingly
plain yet its contents, unkept and
stem broken, are captivating.

Seasons

This land has a history.
Its allays of Pecan trees
once totaled over hundreds.

Now, the trees in full
maturity and grace
stand numbering less than eighty.

The storms and seasons
come and go as the many
who once called this land
their own.

An old tree fort still exists
in portion atop the old cedar
by the oak canopied road.

The many fruit trees are
mature and bring forth
sustenance for the population
of squirrels, rabbits and birds.

This land has a history
that continues as each year passes.

This land is home for
this family season.

Sunday Dinner

Sunday evening.

The remnants of dinner
sogging in the stainless steel sink
and clinging in my over-stuffed
abdomen leave me feeling

full, satisfied, uncomfortable.

At Least I'm not Working

Okay, so I've got a thousand things to do, stores to visit, dry cleaning to pick up. I'll do those on the way to reacquire my children.

I forgot to eat or maybe didn't have time to eat. I accomplished the laundry, house cleaning, and cat feeding.

But now I pace in endless confusion.
What's the cliché?
So little time . . .

I'll prepare something quick for dinner and then do errands. Or, maybe, I should do errands and when I return prepare dinner.

I've got one more load of clothes to fold.
I wanted to weed my garden, but that will have to wait.

Running around like a crazy person
hair unbrushed, disheveled, and nappy
I think to myself.
At least I'm not working.

Ha!

Flaking Polish

I've procrastinated long enough.
My nail tipped fingers, once
bathed in pearlized pink
look as though they were
put through a grinder.

The flaking started two days ago
and has continued so that now
my nails, once flawless,
look unkept and neglected.

Funny how something so simple
as flaking polish mirrors the
more complex inner me.

No More Discussion

I don’t want to talk about it
or give my reasons and excuses.
I just want it all to go away
disappear, evaporate.

Count-down

Tick, tick, tick.
My clock never went tick-tock.
It only ticks as if a bomb.
A count-down as constant,
real, and repetitive as my
nightmares.
My clock ticks.
Hear me. Hear me. Hear me.
It's time.

Savannah

It is a sparkling day
as I sit at my desk writing.
I peer out my window
at a blue jay darting
around in the overgrown grass.

The pecan trees
have dappled the meadow
with large shaded areas
that look quite inviting
for a hammock.

The breeze tickles
the nimble new leafed
branches. The squirrels
use them as springboards
to float forward through air.

The azaleas blooming pink and white frame the view.
Buttercups spot the luscious green with lemon
yellow. I view in impressionistic style a paradise.
One name for Savannah would do here: Monet.

I Too

I passed the old barn while traveling today and
noticed it had a great deal to convey.

Its words traveled through time and
ricochet off the facade of sanity in my mind.

"Notice my windows that once were there. They kept
the bobcats and fox out my lair.

Look at my cedar hair shingles gray and torn. They
kept out bone chilling cold and many a storm.

I used to have four doors, wide and grand. They,
opened wide, could welcome or, shut tight could
defend, but seldom.

These ancient vines that cover my skin
hide many years of torment, and shield me from
wind. So I stand here today after some eighty odd
years speaking in silence of my many rain worn
tears."

I listened to this ancient, wise barn
and hoped that I too, one day,
shall be old, wise, and worn.

Old Pine

Old pine, so brave, so lonely
with arms outstretched
to heaven. You seek.

Old pine, so strong, so lonely
with arms sunk deep
to hell. You seek.

Weathered skin, torn limbs, so lonely
with heart empty
a medium, you seek.

Stay strong, stay firm, stay tall
with others you know
survival they seek.

Old pine, so aged, so kind
with loneliness as company
survive!

Young pine, so small, so innocent
with arms so weak
a friend you seek
old pine.

The Backstop

The brown rusted jagged boards
protect them from the friendly sword,
whose kinship runs with children's play
and swells of laughter drift away.
The passing blurs of colored whispers
jaunt the uninvited one to inquire
and peek to see what fun is passing by,
now, wonderment, sorrow, and sigh.
Inside, the playing continues in spite of no regret.
The sword listens but hasn't been invited yet.

The fence of refuge stands ominously around
a bright green blanket on the ground,
and keeps all safe within its gate,
which no sharpened steel can penetrate.
No patrons of its own,
the sword remains alone.
Splintered weatherworn filter of friendship
has now become the barrier of kinship
neither to let the unknown near,
nor allow the welcomed to fear.

Only the wounds of friendship pending
echo across the backstop without ending,
and remind the sword, whose blade now tarnished,
friendship may not be harnessed.
Still searching through the small parallel sight holes, the
sword wonders how the moles

whose wit and cleverness can overcome
the deadly boards so cumbersome.
But, the fence cannot withstand
the swiftness of a clever plan.

The blade now polished in sterling silver,
glides across the stubby green river,
and places its fist against the gate,
knocks thrice and anticipates.
A friendly face behind the door
questions what it's looking for.
The sword passes a gift of peace
in hopes acceptance will come at least.
A friendship floor follows the squeaking scream of the door.

With polish, pride, and love
the sword sprouts wings like a dove.
With shining white feathers and sparkling eyes, the sword
controls all the skies
and flies over the barrier known,
continuing though not alone.
Continuing, though not alone.

Hang Nail

A tiny bone fragment or stiffened skin
dangles and grabs everything it passes.
Each time it calls for amputation. When
it becomes painful, then I'll listen.

Four Murders

I can't remember exactly what time of year it was except by my clothes, corded pants and sweater. At eleven, a pre-teen with newly permed hair, I thought myself beautiful as I paced in the backyard.

The clothesline, full of freshly washed laundry, hung in three rows ghost dancing in the wind with flat bodies. I stood by the granite bench as Mom held tight to Sugar, a tiny black puff with three rows of teeth, full grown at less than two pounds. Dad was somewhere, I'm sure, because he materialized after the murder.

Husky, a big black and white adoptee with ice eyes lingered close to watch as Mom set sugar on the ground with chicken bone in mouth. A fierce eater, this tiny imp showed no fear as she growled and snipped to protect her last supper.
Husky drew nearer and with one beastly snarl the toothed guillotine fell upon Sugar and broke her neck.

She laid on her side atop the pebbled surface grave. Onlookers stood in shock. I reached down and with one hand lifted the limp defender. Her head bobbled to and fro. Screaming, I laid her down, ran inside, and dove belly down on my bed.

With salt water moistened cheeks, I remembered being six years old when I witnessed Patches' murder by a red and white Ford. Blood flowed from her gapping mouth. As the swirling dirt topped a Kool-aid puddle, I ran screaming down the two-trenched dust road for Mom.

I knew sugar was dead just like I knew Rascal was dead. The sudden thud and jolt of the tires while dad raced from him was far too hard to survive. Rascal chased cars and Dad's truck killed him.

Lying there with hand mask on, I screamed. Just like when Neal, our German Shepherd was kept in our barn, a sort of makeshift hospital.

Neal had been hit and found lying under a neighbor's house. Broken back,
bones bared, flesh ripped, Neal did
not have a chance to recover.
Euthanasia came quick and without
my knowledge.

My memories dissipated as I was suddenly jolted back to the present when I heard voices in the kitchen. Dad had made a call to the Vet and was waiting on a call back.
I wished Husky were dead. The phone rang and I lurched to grab the receiver only to hear Dad say that she was already gone.
"No!" I screamed. I already knew she was dead but hearing Dad say it made it real.

An Interview for Slavery

Oh, I just hate it. It's scheduled for one o'clock. It will be a man. I'm sure of that. He'll call when I'm vomiting over the 'porcelain catchall'.

He'll start with the "How are you?" speech and then thinking himself all-important, the monotone drone will continue for forty-five minutes.

My ear will be numb and my nods of "exactly," "right," and "absolutely" will be so repetitious I'll want to vomit again.

Then the questions for me will start. He'll ask some absurd question about a college course I took five millennia ago and want me to give a full description.

The bull will fly off my tongue like a gecko striking a stinkbug. The tidal wave of stomach acid will swell just listening to me sell myself like a cheap, two-bit whore in a thousand dollar business suit.

The conversation will be a success, by God, as I gear myself up for the close. I'll say just what he wants to hear and manipulate my words into a siren's song.

The close will come with an invitation for employment, and I'll hang up the phone knowing that I've just been made a slave again.

Pinch Pressured

The skin is pressed and indented
by a yoga twisted foot that captures
for only moments my thoughts of
the histories and futures of a day.

There, imbedded on the tender
inner sanctum of my leg, lies a
surface mirror of a woman with a story.

My history is young, but not in my eyes.
Life's battles lost and won and still fighting flitter in
my mind as I stare at the imprint on my leg. Stars,
moons, and suns pressed, perfectly captured by the
encircled chain seem as close and distant as my life's
successes.

The cumbersome ornament of waning youth dangles
as loosely as the path and design of what I thought
was once my future.

Engraved in thought, I watch the imprint slowly fade
while my essence remains.
My thoughts, caused by a pinch pressured ankle
bracelet inside the thigh, deem me very
impressionable.

Incarceration

Piano jazz is playing in the hotel lobby
while I sit in an oversized, modern, plush,
burgundy chair and wait. He's probably
found his way by now. The quest for
being impressive has almost certainly
began. I feel for him, dressed in his
best suit, scarlet tie, vying for a job
to support us.

The couch across from me; a green
velvet embellished with square head
rests is empty and tempting.
I'm the only one in this enormous
welcoming room. Others linger
at the check-in counter, while the
gargantuan marble bar stands empty
of people in these morning hours.

He's probably filling out an application
or answering intrusive questions,
sweating all the while, as I sit here
listening to poorly done jazz.

A couple enters and makes place at a set
of tables and chairs in the far corner.
I imagine what they are doing here.
Both wear brass nametags on their
chests and begin to pull papers out

from nowhere. A meeting in a
hotel lobby of all places, I guess it is
as good a place as any, except for
the public factor.

My make-shift desk, a glass topped
coffee table displays dried flowers,
ferns, leaves and pheasant feathers.
It's not made for writing. It is too
low and my back begins to ache.
I prop my feet up on a round satin
embossed ottoman and revert to
writing on my lap. This is better
and I feel relaxed.

I bet he's not relaxed, up in room
415, being summed up by a total
stranger, who, more than likely,
isn't qualified in such things.

The nametag couple disperse and I'm
alone again. The jazz is so bad. I
long for silence. I hear the clanging
of dishes beneath me and decide
to walk down in search of nourishment.
The four tiers of wide carpeted stairs
lead to a quaint restaurant overlooking
a small duck laced pond.

I'm the only one here, but the jazz
has followed me. In the center of the
pond is a circular fountain, which,
aesthetically, is too large for the pond.

The ducks don't seem to mind it though.

He's still up there, so I'll order
French toast and water, my own
symbolic yet pathetic way of
making a point.

If he's in prison, then so am I.

Stumped

Meltdown at morning.
I sit with fingers poised
and ready to release the
brilliance of words. Only
the thoughts of show don't tell
and don't overwrite stifle.

A stockpile of dog-eared
guidance books and dictionaries
bark the reminder that writing
is not easily learned, and creativity
is an innate talent.

A hardbound spiral journal
of thoughts captured by lead calls.
But, I am not willing to succumb
to the temptation of an archaic quill.

So, I sit here, fingers poised and
brain dripping with an overheated
core waiting for an eruption
of words.

A Day for Resolution

So, this is it,
mediation and contemplation.
The suited masses find their seats
to begin their stare offs.

The leader speaks:
"These are the rules . . ."
Simple enough.

Their side sits with faceless smirks.
Our side, named claimant, goes first.

What's this?
You didn't know our grounds?
Argue that!
The facts are found.

The other side's defense begins:
"She didn't and she did . . ."
Which one is it?

No argument about the facts
we told. No history,
no truth, do the men hold.

The defense of three,
one suited, two which look
as though they should

be on the front nine
with irons in hand
wasting my time.

The leader speaks,
"To your room . . ."
The defense leaves.

Our hired guns begin
to talk of what it is
that made us walk,
and what we want,
this team of two
women worn down
by men's shoes.

So we sit for hours
going back and forth
with ridiculous offers
and pointless discourse.

Early evening sets down
and the women grow weary.
The leader is tired and
our guns are near empty.

The resolution is quickly made.
Take this, or else not
a penny paid.

Don't speak of what
happened here today.
Say only nice things
about the golfers that play

with women's lives.

So this team of claimants
consisting of two
feminine creatures are
directed to live with
the regret that
we lived through this
epithet.

Friends

Mondie was my first true friend. She lived with me while in college. We had a blast. We loved life and all its challenges. We took honesty and friendship to its barriers and beyond. She, I can honestly say is the reason I'm writing this. Her southern twang and gracious smile is intoxicating and contagious. She focused on family then college. She got married to a wonderfully loving man and had two beautiful sons. She's still in college and gripes about it everyday. I don't blame her. She will, no doubt, be a very successful interior designer. Everyone will love her. Everyone does. She's just that sincere. Chicago is her home and I miss her.

Stacey was the second. I met her while working for this horrible little company in Savannah. She was the one that got me started in human resources. What a dreadful career! She loves it. She interprets her career choice as helping people, being involved in their success. Some call her aloof. Please! This girl is intriguing. She is Creole. She would laugh at anyone that asked her, "What are you?" Then she would simply walk away leaving them wondering. A professional with honesty, integrity and true grit, Stacey will go the distance. Neat as a pin! Everything about her was precise. Single, and happy to be that way, Stacey will succeed when all others fail. Lafayette is her home and I miss her.

Meg was the third and last of my true friends thus far. I met Meg while working for the most beautiful place in the world. Only, the people there were less than so. Meg has an innocent aura. She is honest with concern for feelings. She could tell you off and you would thank her for doing it so eloquently. Unbelievable! This girl was put to the test with a man who went mad and left her to raise a child alone. Succeed? Absolutely. Meg's stamina would outlast the sun's. She shines in any occasion. She dreams of owning a shop called Lily Bug. I'm sure she will make that happen. Meg's home is Savannah as is mine.

Friends cherished and admired are the smiles we need when storms of frowns drown us.

The Fake

He arrives in a 1984 Honda
wearing a white linen shirt,
rumpled khakis,
no socks, and loafers.
Gross.

"Hiya goodlookin'."
Yuck.
The sound of that
grotesque, shallow-minded
hello makes me ill.

The smile on his
wrinkled, plastic face
doesn't sell me.

"Okay Honey, we're
just gonna take some pictures
and be out of your hair."
Great! Get out,
you spineless pretender
with the slick tongue.

He wanders through the
house speaking silky phrases
of how great the place looks
and what a great job we
did on the gardens.
Unbelievable!

I can't believe people
like this really exist.

He probably goes home
at night, alone, to a reheated TV
dinner, plops down at a
circa 1973 dinette, and gobbles
without a fork.

There's no shame in fakeness.
So damn me for
being so self-righteous.

I Keep Telling Myself

I've told myself at least a thousand
times that it could be worse.
Life could hand me something
that I'm not prepared for.
I shouldn't whine that the
realtor hasn't sold the house,
or that the deal fell through.
I shouldn't care whether the
company will call with a job offer.

I keep telling myself that the
only thing that matters is my family,
and that all these other problems are
not really problems at all.

I keep telling myself that,
but then I start thinking about the bills,
and the money I haven't got, and the
children's tuition, and the job my husband hates.

I keep telling myself that these things don't matter.
Life is short and one day it won't really matter
anyway.

But then I start thinking about what it is
that I want to do with my life; and what
I can possibly do as a profession;
and who will hire me without discrimination.

I keep telling myself that my children are the only ones I should be concerned about, and that they have their whole lives ahead of them. But then I start wondering if I will be able to pay for their college, and their weddings, and the things that will make them happy, and feel loved.

I keep telling myself that it could be worse.

Pictures

This rag tool, damp with wood polish,
wipes free months of gray dust
off a silver frame.

What a wonderful day that was!
Me, in my Italian satin gown
standing close to the man I
was about to marry. He,
leaned over with his head
rested on mine full clad in
his tuxedo.

That was five years ago and
it seems like yesterday.
I set the simple silver square
frame back between the others
on the table. Its companions of
our children, parents and antique
family I never met stand in disarranged
casual fashion and wait for their
turn to take me back.

Fish fry

Delicious. I pull the steaming white
meat from the bone and slather it
with cheese grits.

Just this morning I caught this fish.
This is the first time for me not to catch and release.
The meat is so tender there's no
need for chewing. I wonder if it
had a family. I'll go see tomorrow.

My Villanelle

To me, there is nothing better than cake.
Emotionless people reign supreme.
Two layers are better and that's what I bake.

No, I don't share you see, I only take.
That wasn't me, it must have been a dream.
To me, there is nothing better than cake.

No, I am the real McCoy not a fake.
Yes, I know love is everyone's main theme.
Two layers are better and that's what I bake.

Oh, I see you think our love is at stake,
but only when you complicate my scheme.
To me, there is nothing better than cake.

I have been hurt by love so don't rake
me now. Be simple, unlike me, and dream.
Two layers are better and that's what I bake.

The outer and inner person I make.
The latter outshines even the sun's beam.
To me there is nothing better than cake.
Two layers are better and that's what I bake.

Ode to Mildred

It's been called many things.
But for me, her name is Mildred.
She, I'm assuming its female,
reeks havoc on my life and
everyone around me, poor people.
My life light is sucked out by an
invisible vacuum that is connected
to my [redacted] once a month.
The weight of pain and misery
grows stronger. One
even thinks I should be used to
her by now, in my thirties. Please!
[redacted] Eve!

Escape

A small world, encircled by glass atop
a black marble pedestal, sits between
me and my view of the green wall.
Inside this snow world is where
I should be. I wish I could bore a
tiny hole into my winter water land
and slide inside.

The Offering

Oh my God! She did it again,
my sweet little calico;
black, orange, and white with
white paws and hidden claws.

She comes and goes through the cracked door. On
the orange, Mexican tiled floor she terrorizes a
creature with webbed feet, no eyes, and a snout nose.
This beast scurries in blindness avoiding the scythes
of death.

I grab a towel, so that my hands don't
touch this sacrificial lamb, and take
it to the woods, so that it may be safe.

The other day she lay a headless lizard
belly up outside the cracked door.
Unnoticed for hours, the ant-ridden corpse graced the
wooden deck.

Each morn before the feedings begin
she brings me a new offering.
Be it lizard, snake, or mole.

Drowning

I want to be a part of it, the forum, and the critique.
I post and I post, but only get
minimum response.

Must be, that I suck. Or, the members are in some sort
of click where they just look for familiar names to
praise and provide help. I just keep posting in the sea,
arms flailing around grasping for something,
anything.

The sharks aren't even circling. Must be, that I suck,
or possibly too good to critique? Nope.
It's the former, but I'm not so sure of it.

Without Warning

All of a sudden the sensation
hits me as my mouth opens
wide in a silent scream
and inhale.

My arms outstretch as my
muscles tighten in rigid vibrato.
Straight legged, I pose in
Rigor mortis state for
the yawn and stretch.

Drought

The earth is parched
as a sun dried tomato.
The garden is dehydrated and dying.

The sun sets heavy
over what was once a green meadow dappled with
buttercup flowers.

The meadow, a brownish olive, is
too harsh to walk on with bare feet.

I pamper my seedlings with daily waterings.
This morning they but withered and died.

Do nothing, but rain I pray.
No rain, no rain, no rain.
All death and decay.

Driving in the Rain

Back and forth
and back and forth.
Repeating over and over
wiping off the skies secretions.

Faster and faster in synchronized rhythm the swiping
motion rids us of nothing, but merely smears and
pushes aside the gravity driven water.

Now, drizzle, drizzle,
Wipers are on delay mode.
Swipe, pause, drizzle.
Swipe, pause, drizzle.

No more.

On Love

Paris in July

River Seine is a murky green.
A gentle breeze saunters
through the hats of trees
while art vendors set up their booths.

I wander through the maze
to the Sacra Cur.
Up and down the bricked streets
I pass whimsical stores, gypsies, and freaks.
I find a table for two at a café
and sip espresso.

Exhaling in the relaxation of
Paris in July, I note that
no other city will do
for one who wishes she was two.

Settled

So I'm now domesticated.
It's official.
The knot is tied.
The children are born.

Our dogs, all three, bounce
around each other in delight.
Our cats, lay atop our
furniture all day long.

Our love, though once
new and fresh, is several
years old. But, I still get
butterflies when I see you.

I still miss you when you
are gone. I still remember
how we first met on a plane
to London.

I feel secure, sentimental and
settled with you.

True

I breathe in life,
happiness and you.
Heart beats for nothing but
your love so true.

You Are

All the wonders of the world,
you create them.
All the great stories told,
you, my darling, write them.
All the kings and valiant heroes,
you teach them.
All the wild and vicious wolves,
you, my dear, tame them.
All the unexplained mysteries,
you unveil them.
All the trials and problems in life,
you, my heart, solve them.
All the starving sufferers,
you feed them.
All the lost and scared,
you, my soul, find them.
All the historic brutal battles,
you win them.
All the sorrowful, pitiful souls,
you, my solace, comfort them.
All the questions of children,
you humor them.
All the illness and misery,
you, my miracle, cure them.
All the laughter and joy in life,
you cause them.
All the depth of love and adoration,
you are them.
All of everything good in perpetuity,
you are.

Gaze Only by Distance

I smell of rose oil
placed there by me
to call him near as the
humid air hangs heavily
upon my breast.

I long to hold my love
whose breath whispers soothing words.

Crystal blue as brilliant topaz
are his beautiful eyes.

His smile commands notice
by sincerity and genuineness.

Brown silken locks lay upon his brow, with matching
majestic furrow around his mouth.

His succulent lips
are pure plump and ripe.
I took a nibble once long ago and
became intoxicated by his kiss.

His hands large and strong
can hold me like no other.

His stature is as monumental
as an ancient Egyptian statue.

His gait is both
powerful and humble.

Truth be known, he's a living god, one that the Greeks would have idolized in gold.

His love is as eternal as the universe. I have found him and with greed I will keep him forever. I will not share him or lose him or hurt him ever.

He's mine.
Gaze only by distance.
There is no other as perfect as he. I feel for all women who cannot feel his ecstasy.

Lemonade Serenade

I was asked once to describe love.
Unable to capture in mere words
at a moments notice, the answer,
I took to long rumination.
Love, to me, is like:

a late May, early evening shower
that brings a cooling breeze
and rolling thunder,

lying on a hammock
under the cover of trees
dripping with Spanish moss
listening to the crickets' song,

taking your first bite of Granny's
seven layer chocolate cake,

sipping chilled lemonade after
working for hours weeding your
garden in the hot sun,

walking on the edge of the ocean
as the moon caresses the water
and the warm sand covers your toes,

hearing the first cry of the
precious child you carried in your womb,

seeing the smile of acceptance
on the face of one adored,

feeling the torment in
absence of those gone before,

standing mid mountain stream
with a record-breaking rainbow
dangling on a self-tied fly,

finishing the last page of
your favorite book for the tenth time,

and playing the violin so well that it sings.

My answer in short:

Love is knowing the worst thing
that life could ever hand you
is to never have known what love is.

Corded Love

She cradles my child as if her own
and loves her child that now is grown.

She carries my pain as if to share
my losses in life and my despair.

She smiles so gently and sincere
giving approval and removing my fear.

A true monument of devotion I have seen the teacher,
the mentor, the mother supreme.

No words writ can simply describe how I feel for her,
my mother truelove.

We share one heart and thus one soul
all our dreams, wishes, and goals.

When they cut our binding cord at birth,
our love grew stronger and then I knew
no other person on this vast earth
could come close to what this woman's worth.

If fate should take me from her side,
I'll walk the pillowed sky far and wide
and wait for her forever. Our corded love shall erase
the birth sever and with our others in heaven we'll
always be together.

On Childhood

A Concert for One

She tinkles and hammers
the notes alone
while singing her nursery rhymes.

The notes are pounded out
with determination and might.
Eighty-eight keys of black and white
create endless entertainment
and three-year-old delight.

Two Sisters Converse

"You can have this one.
You don't have enough.
So! Mine can reach long distance.
So! See! Well, how do
you like my garden?
Do you want me to
give you an Indian red burn?
I mean a rose garden.
Sorry. Huckleberry.
Girls, girls, girls."

Singing begins:

"It isn't how you sing it, see:
Shambiya, shambiya, shambiya.
Hey, is that an old fashioned beetle?"

Green Chair

Nineteen-fifties style and design
this child's chair with plastic
seat cover fashioned to look
like green marble.

Two black wooden steps assist
in climbing to the high throne.

This child wishes to climb
without steps but with
mother's hand.

Stay

See the innocent porcelain that I create.
It shines a snowy peach.
I mold and mold.

I fashion the fragile finery, as if she were I. I place silken ribbons round and round penetrating my porcelain with devoted kisses.

I cover this priceless frailty with strength to hold strong.
I guide the kiln to warm the soul.
I comfort this jewel of mine and hold it to my breast as the years go by.

My porcelain grows strong with passion and forbearance.
Glistening blue are the eyes of my doll.
I mourn and mourn.

The solace of my breast is but a wisp of comfort, for soon, years will take my porcelain away.
I cherish.

Though away, my doll may need me some day, so waiting, hoping, here,
I'll stay.

Faith

Question not my reason for shedding tears,
while the ground is freshly tilled still.
Tempt not my heart to feel less these: my fears,
for I alone must accept Devine will.
Question not why He has taken my child,
while her mother's arms long to caress.
This mother has not future reconcile,
fate holds doom to a childless mother's breast.
Question not my womb now empty of life
while she lay asleep in loneliest death.
I have all rights to sink in deepest strife
and question this God whose will took her breath.
See now my reasons are significant,
thus I remain always belligerent.

Seasons Losses

I lost her in summer and life was gone
and fall came
cool mornings, dropping leaves, and sorrow
cover me
pain

Another waits her own return
and I still yearn
her eyes, her face, her love
abscond me
pain

I lost her in fall and life was gone
and winter came
cold air, dark nights, and loneliness
pierce me
pain

Another waits her mother's return
and I still yearn
her eyes, her face, her love
escape me
pain

I lost her in winter and life was gone
and spring came
warm days, cool breeze, and loneliness
surround me
pain

Another awaits his wife's return
and I still yearn
her eyes, her face, her love
left me
pain

I lost her in spring and rebirth is found
and summer came
sweet giggles, small hands, precious eyes
love me
joy

I lost her in summer and found her again
and life came
small angel, fly free, so precious
protect me
joy

I lost her last summer and now I find
joy through another
I return
alive!

Clunk

Clunk. Clunk. Clunk.
To be four again and
dressed in Mom's blue
satin heels with long strands
of make-believe pearls that
hang down to my knees.

To be four again with a cigar
box overflowing with crayons
trying to find the perfect pink
to color the flower I just drew.

To be four again.

Nonsense

Pitter-patter. Screeching laughter.
Ten fingers and ten toes tap lightly
on the oak floor as the singer is fat.

Goose golden, rod broken, laugh
tightly as a fisherman's knot.

Up and down and in and out the
whispers of ferns dot the rabbit
hole. Downtrodden, froth rotten
as the witch's brew. Hang dangling
as a bell banging in the clear wind.
Push petals, wheels turning over
a pebbled path. Bud blooming,
tiny fingers pluck the petals one by
one. He loves me.

My Fancy World

Where turtles run fast and
where birds swim,
I love when they all win.
Fish can fly and
soar high.
Frogs walk on their hind legs
and play with each other .
Trees would talk and
grab you.
Crabs would walk backwards instead of sideways.
Cats would go to school and
ace every test.
Dogs would train people to protect and
do tricks.
Snakes wouldn't slither but have two little legs in the
back and walk around.
Hippos would kiss and kiss all day long.
Crocs and gators would be vegetarians.
Deer would be warlike aggressive.
People would be in pet shops for sale.
And that's what would be in my fancy world.

Georgia Ann Bell
Age 11

Yes I am

Yes I am! I told you so!
It's mine, I said. So, let it go.

Give it back. Let me see!
It's mine, I said. So, let me be!

Yes I am! I told you so!
Don't break it! Don't touch it! NO!

I'll take it! I'll break it!
See, I told you so!

Oh, it's yours. You take it! Here you go!

Open the Door

Open the door and see what's inside.
Turn the doorknob and open it wide.
What? No Monsters? Nothing to hide.
Don't be so silly and worry so much.
You'd think there was a lion or tiger or such
hiding in your closet with fangs large and sharp.
We'll turn on the light and open your toy box.
See, nothing inside except toys and a few odd socks.
Open the door and see what's inside.
Only your imagination to make you run hide.

Comeback

One day, when I was one year old,
my sister died. I don't know how,
but all I know is that I want her to
comeback.

Her name is Faith and she made me feel
as if for the first time someone looked up
to me.

My mom doesn't talk about it,
but I sometimes cry just thinking
about her.

She is buried in Savannah in Bonaventure
cemetery.

Ten years ago mom put a small doll on
the stone.

I cry and cry every time I am there.
I sometimes feel as if a whole chunk
of my heart is missing and it hurts.

Even though that was ten years ago,
I still remember.
Even though I was young,
tears filled my eyes.

I never saw her.
I never gazed upon her face.

Dad was really excited that she
was on the way but that changed.
Mom was the saddest of us all.
She cried more and more.

I also don't like to talk about her.
I think she died right after birth.

I don't know why God chose her.
I don't know why I miss her so much.
I hardly knew her.

I shall see her again,
but that is in a long time.

I am the only one who ever speaks
of Faith.

It is hard when you want someone
to comeback.

Georgia Ann Bell
Age 11

Samone Norsworthy, born in Savannah, Georgia, began writing poetry as a child. Her interest in writing evolved into an intense passion while attending Armstrong Atlantic State University in Savannah. She lives in Savannah with her husband and two daughters.

Printed in the United States
5416